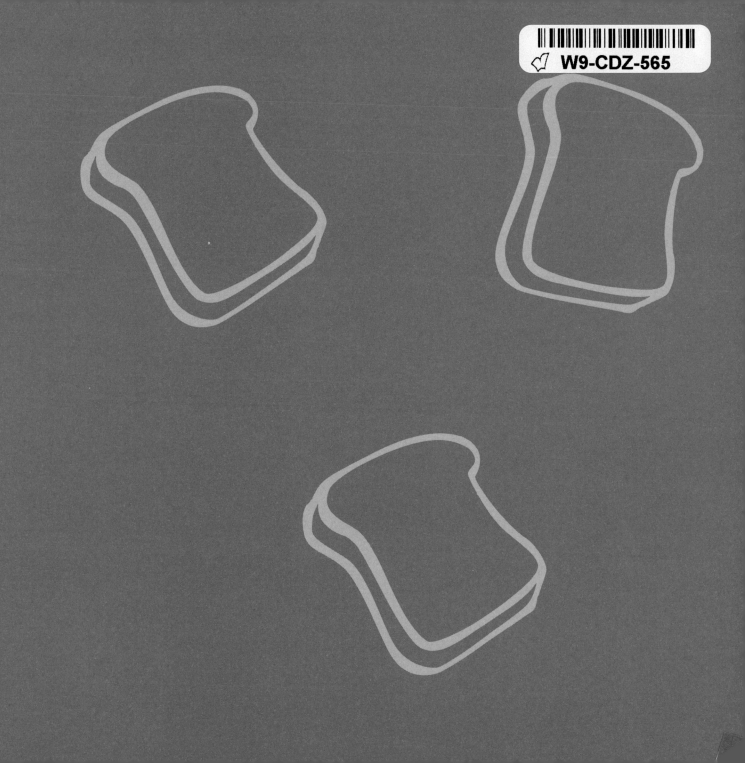

French Toast

French Toast

Sweet & Savory Dishes for Every Meal

Donna Kelly

Photographs by Joyce Oudkerk Pool

Gibbs Smith, Publisher
TO ENRICH AND INSPIRE HUMANKIND

Salt Lake City | *Charleston* | *Santa Fe* | *Santa Barbara*

First Edition
12 11 10 09 08   10 9 8 7 6 5 4 3 2 1

Text © 2008 Donna Kelly
Photographs © 2008 Joyce Oudkerk Pool

Published by
Gibbs Smith, Publisher
P.O. Box 667
Layton, Utah 84041

Orders: 1.800.835.4993
www.gibbs-smith.com

Printed and bound in Hong Kong

Library of Congress Cataloging-in-Publication Data
Kelly, Donna.
  French toast : sweet & savory dishes for every meal / Donna Kelly.—1st ed.
      p. cm.
   ISBN-13: 978-1-4236-0248-4
   ISBN-10: 1-4236-0248-X
  1. French toast. I. Title.
   TX770.F73K45 2008
   641.8'15—dc22
                        2007035083

This book is lovingly dedicated to families everywhere and to the tradition of sharing delicious meals—whether breakfast, lunch or dinner, in unity and love.

Contents

Acknowledgments

This book is published with thanks to the many taste testers who frequent my home and provide frank and helpful critiques of my culinary experiments. I am most grateful to my daughter Kate and her wonderful husband Neil; my daughter Amy and her sweet husband Chris; my sons Jake and Matt and their entourages always eager to sample my foods; my daughter Anne, for her culinary and other advice; and most of all my eternal companion Jim, the most patient and supportive husband on the planet.

All About French Toast

French toast is one of the oldest and most popular breakfast foods. It is derived from the original French recipe *pain perdu,* or "lost bread." It started as an ingenious way to use stale or "lost bread" by dipping it in an egg and milk mixture and cooking it. The concept lends itself to an almost infinite variety of flavors and versions—all easy enough to make even the average cook an instant gourmet.

Because French toast is so easy and convenient, I became its biggest fan when my children were small. As time went by, it became a family favorite and eventually crept into our family fare at meals other than break-fast. I found that, with a little experimenting, the possibilities with French toast were endless. Different types of breads opened up whole new worlds of flavors and combi-nations. Some of the most delicious mingled tastes were not the standard French toast with maple syrup, but rather a savory blend of cheeses, onion and bits of meat. It was almost like a simplified and fail-safe version of a soufflé. Now French toast forms the base for many hearty and flavorful meals at our table, and I hope it does at your table too.

Breads

The term "day-old" is used throughout this book and is commonly used in the cooking world to mean bread that is dried out. This is important in French toast recipes, as fresh bread is too soggy and falls apart while cooking. Dry bread absorbs the egg and milk mixture better than fresh bread, which is what makes the classic French toast texture.

The best method for drying fresh bread is to set slices on a wire rack and then leave it out for several hours or overnight so that air can circulate on both sides of the bread slices. In a pinch, bread can be dried out in the oven by placing the slices directly on the oven racks and baking for 20 minutes at 200 degrees. You can also toast bread in a toaster for several seconds, but watch closely so bread does not brown or then it can't be used.

Generally, the quality of the bread determines the quality of the French toast recipe. Try specialty breads baked in local bakeries. Cinnamon swirls, cheese-topped and other breads with added flavors will add character to your French toast recipes.

Cooking

Try experimenting with the quantity of eggs and milk for dipping the bread and find the proportions you like best. The general rule is that there should be 3 large eggs to 1 cup of milk. The standard proportion can be varied, depending on the individual recipe, but the more eggs you use, the more dense and custard-like the texture will be. Also, avoid adding large amounts of sugar to the egg mixture as it will burn when cooking the French toast in the frying pan.

French toast must be cooked one slice at a time, or in a pan big enough that multiple slices don't touch while cooking. It works best to use a nonstick sauté pan, but to make sure the French toast doesn't stick, spray the pan with a little nonstick cooking spray before cooking each slice. And, generally, the pan should be covered with a lid while cooking French toast to ensure that the middle is cooked through. To keep individual slices warm, place them on a wire rack on a baking sheet in a warm oven. Or, toast the slices lightly in a toaster just before serving to reheat.

When cooking French toast casseroles, make sure they have soaked for several hours or overnight in the refrigerator before baking. This allows the bread and egg mixture to infuse thoroughly and helps to develop a custard-like texture. To ensure even cooking, always bring casseroles to room temperature, which takes about 30 minutes, before baking.

Garnishes

French toast, like pancakes or waffles, can be garnished to make a more stunning and delightful presentation. Try adding some of the following garnishes to make your toast look gourmet!

Fresh fruits—diced, sliced, or whole— make colorful and flavorful toppings. Using any fruit that is in season will add that extra special taste to your toast.

Powdered sugar is an elegant garnish that, when sprinkled through a sieve or a paper doily, makes a unique pattern for family and friends to enjoy.

Try garnishing sweet French toasts with your favorite chopped nuts or crushed cereals and then drizzle syrup over the top. The sweet taste combined with the crunchy texture is rich and delicious.

For savory French toasts, sprinkling grated cheeses or minced parsley not only adds taste, but also adds refreshing color . Add minced or diced peppers or thinly sliced or julienned green onions to complement southwest style toasts.

Storing

Cooked French toast slices are easy to store. Individual slices should be cooled and placed in a ziplock bag, separated by a piece of wax paper. They can be stored in the refrigerator up to three or four days, or can be frozen up to two weeks. To reheat, simply bake at 350 degrees on a baking sheet for a few minutes or toast in the toaster until heated through. Serve with syrup or your favorite toppings.

French toast casseroles are best eaten straight from the oven because they are sometimes difficult to store due to the large dish in which they are usually baked. However, they can be covered and refrigerated for up to three days and then reheated in the oven at 350 degrees. Warm until heated thoroughly and slightly crisp around the edges. Serve with syrup or your favorite toppings.

Many recipes can be made ahead of time and stored in the refrigerator until ready to use. Just remove from the refrigerator about 30 minutes before baking and bring to room temperature—this helps it to bake evenly.

Creating Your Own French Toast Recipes

Once you have experimented with the recipes in this book, you will be ready to venture out and create your own French toast favorites. Try using cooked savory French toast slices as a base for your favorite cooked vegetables or meats and sauces. Bake casseroles using soaked French bread cubes tossed with your family's favorite foods. Use fruit breads and slices of dense cakes to form a base for decadent dessert with sweet toppings. Be bold and use new spices and flavorings with plain breads to give your toast an appetizing twist. And always remember, the possibilities are endless!

Family Favorites

The Classic

THIS BASIC RECIPE CAN'T BE BEAT—MOIST AND FLUFFY ON THE INSIDE,
CRISPY ON THE OUTSIDE.

1 cup milk
1/4 cup flour
3 large eggs
2 teaspoons vanilla
1/2 teaspoon salt
6 slices day-old firm white bread
Butter

In a pie pan or other shallow pan, whisk together milk and flour; whisk in eggs, vanilla and salt. Soak each bread slice in egg mixture for 10 to 20 seconds on each side, or until just soaked through. Heat a little butter in a small frying pan over medium-high heat. Cover and cook soaked bread in the pan 2 to 3 minutes on each side, or until lightly browned. Serve with butter and syrup, or try the Old-Fashioned Buttermilk Syrup on page 125. Makes 6 slices.

Santa Fe Railroad

SERVED ON THE SANTA FE RAILROAD LINE IN FRONTIER AMERICA, THIS VARIATION OF THE FAMOUS RECIPE COMBINES TWO BREAKFAST FAVORITES—CORN FLAKES AND FRENCH TOAST—INTO ONE BREAKFAST DELIGHT!

4 large eggs
2 cups milk
2 tablespoons vanilla
1/2 teaspoon salt
4 cups crushed corn flakes
2 tablespoons powdered sugar
1 teaspoon cinnamon
8 slices day-old firm white bread
Butter

In a pie pan or other shallow pan, whisk together eggs, milk, vanilla and salt. In a bowl, mix together corn flakes, powdered sugar and cinnamon and then spread on a plate. Soak bread in egg mixture on each side for about 1 minute. Press soaked bread into corn flake mixture. Heat a little butter in a small frying pan over medium heat. Cover and cook soaked bread in the pan 2 to 3 minutes on each side, or until lightly browned and crisp. Serve with your favorite syrup. Makes 8 slices.

Waffle Style

THE COMBINATION OF WAFFLES AND FRENCH TOAST CREATES A CRISPY CRUST THAT HOLDS AS MUCH BUTTER AND SYRUP AS YOUR HEART DESIRES.

4 large eggs
1 cup milk
1 teaspoon vanilla
1 tablespoon sugar
1/2 teaspoon salt
8 (1-inch-thick) slices day-old challah or French bread

Preheat a waffle iron and spray generously with nonstick cooking spray. In a pie pan or other shallow pan, whisk together eggs, milk, vanilla, sugar and salt. Dip bread slices in egg mixture until well soaked. Cook slices in the waffle iron one at a time until lightly brown. Serve with warm syrup, powdered sugar and/or fresh fruit as a garnish. Makes 8 slices.

Healthy Start

THE PERFECT MARRIAGE OF HEALTHY YOGURT AND FLAVORFUL FRUIT—A
GREAT WAY TO START YOUR DAY.

1 container (6 ounces) low-fat
  yogurt, any flavor
1/4 cup water
2 egg whites
6 slices day-old multigrain bread
3 teaspoons olive oil
Fresh Fruit Purée (see page 124)

If yogurt has large chunks of fruit, blend with the water in a blender. In a pie pan or other shallow pan, whisk together the yogurt, water and egg whites; dip bread on both sides in the yogurt mixture. Heat a small frying pan to medium-high heat and spread 1/2 teaspoon olive oil in the pan. Cover and cook soaked bread in the pan 2 to 3 minutes on both sides, or until lightly browned. Add 1/2 teaspoon oil to pan when cooking each bread slice. Serve with Fresh Fruit Purée or syrup, if desired. Makes 6 slices.

Elvis' Favorite

ELVIS LOVED GRILLED PEANUT BUTTER AND BANANA SANDWICHES, SO WE'RE SURE THIS WOULD BE HIS BREAKFAST OF CHOICE.

1 cup milk

3 large eggs

1/2 teaspoon salt

8 tablespoons creamy
    peanut butter

8 thin slices day-old firm
    white bread

Butter

1 large banana, mashed

4 teaspoons honey

In a pie pan or other shallow pan, whisk together milk, eggs and salt. Spread 2 tablespoons peanut butter on one side of 4 bread slices and then soak dry side of each slice in the egg mixture for 10 to 20 seconds, or until soaked through. Heat a little butter in a small frying pan over medium heat. Place soaked bread in pan with peanut butter facing up. Spread one side of remaining bread slices with one-fourth of the mashed banana. Drizzle each with 1 teaspoon honey. Soak dry side of each slice in egg mixture for 10 to 20 seconds, or until soaked through. Place soaked bread, banana side down, on top of other slice already in pan. Press with a spatula so the two slices stick together. Cover and cook for 2 to 3 minutes on each side, or until lightly browned. Serve sandwich warm and with syrup for dipping, if desired. Makes 4 servings.

Crunchy Graham Dipping Sticks

THE SWEET CRUNCHY GRAHAM CRACKER COATING WILL APPEAL TO EVERYONE IN YOUR FAMILY, YOUNG AND OLD.

6 slices lightly toasted
   Texas-style toast (or other
   firm, thick white bread)
1 cup heavy cream
2 large eggs
1 teaspoon vanilla
1/2 teaspoon salt
9 graham crackers
Canola oil

Cut each bread slice lengthwise into four sticks. In a pie pan or other shallow pan, mix together the cream, eggs, vanilla and salt. Whirl the graham crackers in a food processor until they are fine crumbs. Spread graham cracker crumbs on a plate. Dip sticks, one by one, into egg mixture and then press into cracker crumbs, coating thoroughly. Heat a little oil in a small frying pan. Cover and cook sticks over medium heat 2 to 3 minutes on each side, or until lightly browned. Cool until warm enough to handle. Serve with a side of syrup and use your fingers to dip. Makes 24 sticks.

Variation: *Spread oil on a baking sheet and place all coated sticks on sheet. Bake for 8 minutes at 425 degrees. Turn over and bake another 3 minutes.*

Surprise Inside

THESE YUMMY BREAKFAST SANDWICHES ARE FILLED WITH SWEETENED CREAM CHEESE!

4 large eggs
1/2 cup cream
1 tablespoon cinnamon
1/4 cup sugar
2 teaspoons vanilla, divided
1/2 teaspoon salt
12 thin slices day-old firm
    white bread
8 ounces cream cheese, softened
1 tablespoon pure maple syrup
Butter
Decadent Vanilla Cream Syrup
    (see page 120)

In a bowl, whisk together eggs, cream, cinnamon, sugar, 1 teaspoon vanilla and salt until frothy. Pour half of the egg mixture into a 9 x 13-inch pan. Place 6 slices bread in pan, completely filling pan. Using a hand mixer, mix together cream cheese, maple syrup and remaining vanilla. Place 2 heaping tablespoons cream cheese mixture on the center of each bread slice in the pan. Place remaining bread slices on top. Press firmly so that cream cheese flattens slightly but doesn't ooze out. Pour remaining egg mixture over top and then let soak for 10 minutes. Heat a little butter in a small frying pan over medium-high heat. Using a wide spatula, remove French toast sandwich from soaking pan and place in frying pan. Cover and cook 2 to 3 minutes on each side, or until lightly browned. Serve drizzled with Decadent Vanilla Cream Syrup. Makes 6 servings.

One-Eyed Bandit

COOK YOUR EGG WITH YOUR FRENCH TOAST IN THIS TWIST ON THE CLASSIC
FAVORITE FROM THE '50S.

1 cup milk
1/4 cup flour
9 large eggs, divided
2 teaspoons vanilla
1/2 teaspoon salt
6 slices day-old firm white bread
Butter

In a pie pan or other shallow pan, whisk together milk and flour; whisk in 3 eggs, vanilla and salt. Cut a hole in the center of each bread slice with a 3-inch round cookie cutter. Soak each bread slice and the removed circle for 10 to 20 seconds on each side, or until just soaked through. Heat a little butter in a small frying pan over medium-high heat. Place soaked bread in pan and crack an egg into the center hole. Cover and cook the bread slice and removed circle 2 to 3 minutes on each side, or until lightly browned. Place the small circle slightly off-center, and just covering part of the egg. Serve with butter and syrup. Makes 6 slices.

Specialty

Eggs Benedict Stacks

THIS EASY BUT ELEGANT TWIST ON AN OLD BREAKFAST TRADITION LOOKS AND TASTES GOURMET.

6 large eggs, divided

2/3 cup milk

1/4 teaspoon salt

8 English muffins, cut in half

Easy Blender Hollandaise Sauce
  (see page 124)

8 slices Canadian bacon

In a pie pan or other shallow pan, whisk together 2 eggs, milk and salt with a fork. Soak English muffin halves for 1 or 2 minutes on each side. Heat a small frying pan sprayed with nonstick cooking spray over medium-high heat. Cover and cook soaked muffin halves one at a time for about 2 minutes on each side, or until lightly browned. Place cooked muffin halves on a plate and set aside. Cook the remaining eggs individually as desired. To assemble stacks, toast 2 muffin halves in toaster for 1 minute, or until lightly crisp. Place 1 muffin half on a plate and then spread with a tablespoon of Easy Blender Hollandaise Sauce. Place 2 slices Canadian bacon over sauce. Place a cooked egg on top and then drizzle generously with more sauce. Lay remaining muffin half on top and serve. Makes 4 servings.

Chai Latte

TRY THIS MODERN CAFÉ FLAVOR IN AN UPDATED FRENCH TOAST!

1 cup milk

3 tablespoons instant powdered
   chai latte drink mix

3 large eggs

8 (1-inch-thick) slices day-old
   challah or French bread

Butter

In a pie pan or other shallow pan, whisk together milk and latte powder; whisk in eggs. Soak each bread slice for 10 to 20 seconds on each side, or until just soaked through. Heat a little butter in a small frying pan over medium-low heat. Cover and cook soaked bread in the pan 2 to 3 minutes on each side, or until lightly browned. (The sugar in the powdered drink mix will burn if the pan is too hot, so watch the heat closely and lower as necessary while cooking.) Serve with butter and syrup. Makes 8 slices.

Orange Sunshine

FORGET HAVING A GLASS OF ORANGE JUICE—GET YOUR CITRUS FIX WITH THIS TASTY CITRUS FRENCH TOAST.

1 cup orange sherbet, melted
4 large eggs
1/2 cup milk
8 ounces cream cheese, softened
2 tablespoons frozen orange juice
  concentrate
16 (1/2-inch-thick) slices day-old
  French bread
8 tablespoons orange marmalade
Butter
Citrus Sunshine Syrup
  (see page 126)

In a pie pan or other shallow pan, whisk together the sherbet, eggs and milk. Using a hand mixer, mix together the cream cheese and orange juice concentrate in a bowl. Spread one side of 8 bread slices with 1 tablespoon cream cheese mixture. Spread 1 tablespoon marmalade on top of cream cheese. Soak dry side of bread slices in egg mixture for about 30 seconds. Heat a little butter in a small frying pan over medium heat. Place bread in pan, soaked side down. Spread one side of each remaining bread slice with 1 tablespoon cream cheese and then soak dry side in egg mixture for about 30 seconds. Place on top of slices in pan, cream cheese side down, forming a cream cheese and marmalade center. Cover and cook about 2 minutes on each side, or until lightly browned. Serve hot with Citrus Sunshine Syrup. Makes 8 slices.

Stuffed Croissant

THIS IS A DELICIOUS AND EASY RECIPE THAT IS ELEGANT ENOUGH TO
SERVE TO COMPANY.

2 eggs
1 cup milk
2 teaspoons vanilla
12 medium-sized
  day-old croissants
8 ounces cream cheese, softened
1/4 cup powdered sugar
1 pint strawberries, thinly sliced
Butter

In a bowl, whisk together the eggs, milk and vanilla; pour into a 9 x 13-inch baking pan. Slice each croissant almost completely through horizontally. With a hand mixer, mix together the cream cheese and powdered sugar. Spread a layer of cream cheese mixture on the inside surface of each croissant. Place strawberry slices over cream cheese mixture and press lightly to secure. Close the croissants and place in the 9 x 13-inch pan; soak each side for 2 to 3 minutes. Melt a little butter in a small frying pan and then place croissant in pan. Cover and cook about 1 minute on each side, or until lightly browned. Serve immediately sprinkled with powdered sugar. Makes 6 servings.

Variation: *Replace strawberries with any fruit, such as peaches, kiwis, or raspberries.*

Cinnamon Craving

AND YOU THOUGHT RAISIN BREAD COULDN'T GET ANY YUMMIER!

1 cup milk
1/4 cup flour
3 large eggs
2 teaspoons vanilla
1/2 teaspoon salt
1/2 teaspoon cinnamon
6 slices day-old cinnamon
   raisin bread
Butter
Cinnamon Cream Syrup (see
   page 125)

In a pie pan or other shallow pan, whisk together the milk and flour; whisk in eggs, vanilla, salt, and cinnamon. Soak each bread slice for 10 to 20 seconds on each side, or until just soaked through. Heat a little butter in a frying pan over medium heat. Cook soaked bread in pan 1 to 2 minutes on each side, or until lightly browned. Serve with butter and Cinnamon Cream Syrup. Makes 6 slices.

Dairy Free

WITH TOFU AND SOY MILK, THIS RECIPE TASTES GREAT AND IS EXTRA HEALTHY!

1/2 cup firm tofu
1 cup vanilla soy milk
1 teaspoon vanilla
1 teaspoon cinnamon
1/4 teaspoon turmeric
8 slices day-old dairy-free bread

Mix all ingredients except the bread in a blender; pour into a pie pan. Dip bread slices in mixture for a few seconds on each side, soaking evenly. Heat a frying pan sprayed with non-stick cooking spray to medium heat. Cover and cook soaked bread 2 to 3 minutes on each side, or until lightly browned and firm. Serve with syrup or other desired toppings. Makes 8 slices.

Brie and Apple Stuffed

TRY THIS GOURMET COMBINATION OF CREAMY BRIE AND CRUNCHY APPLES FOR AN EXTRA FLAVORFUL BRUNCH.

3 large eggs
1 cup milk
1 teaspoon vanilla
1/2 teaspoon salt
1/4 teaspoon cinnamon
1/8 teaspoon nutmeg
12 (1/2-inch-thick) slices day-old
  French bread
8 ounces brie, thinly sliced
  (outer coating removed)
1 Golden Delicious apple, peeled
  and cut into 1/8-inch-thick slices
Butter

In a pie pan or other shallow pan, whisk together the eggs, milk, vanilla, salt and spices. Cover one side of 6 bread slices with brie and apple slices. Place remaining bread slices on top to form sandwiches and then press together slightly to seal. Dip sandwiches in egg mixture for 30 seconds on each side. Melt some butter in a small frying pan over medium-high. Cover and cook each sandwich for 2 to 3 minutes on each side, or until lightly browned. Serve hot with syrup. Makes 6 servings.

Tropical Paradise

WHAT COULD TASTE MORE TROPICAL THAN COCONUT, PINEAPPLE AND RUM?

4 large eggs

1 can (14 ounces) coconut
   milk, shaken

1/2 cup apricot pineapple jam

1 teaspoon rum flavoring

4 cups corn flakes

1 cup diced macadamia nuts

1 cup sweetened coconut

8 slices day-old firm white bread

Butter

In a blender, mix together the eggs, coconut milk, jam and rum flavoring; pour mixture into a pie pan or other shallow pan. In a food processor, pulse together corn flakes, nuts and coconut until they are coarse crumbs, and then spread on a plate. Soak each bread slice in egg mixture for about 1 minute on each side. Press soaked bread into coconut mixture on each side. Melt a little butter in a small frying pan over medium heat and then place coated bread into pan. Cover and cook 2 to 3 minutes on each side, or until lightly browned and crisp. Serve with your favorite syrup. Makes 8 slices.

Banana Supreme

BANANA BREAD STUFFED WITH A SWEET ALMOND CREAM AND MORE BANANAS REALLY HITS THE SPOT.

8 (1/2-inch-thick) slices day-old
   firm banana bread
4 tablespoons cream cheese,
   softened
1 teaspoon almond extract
2 tablespoons powdered sugar
1/2 cup sweetened condensed milk
3 eggs
1 teaspoon vanilla
2 ripe bananas, thinly sliced

Spread bread slices out on a baking sheet and let stand to dry for a few hours or overnight, turning over at least once. With a hand mixer, mix together the cream cheese, almond extract and powdered sugar. In a pie pan or other shallow pan, whisk together the condensed milk, eggs and vanilla. Soak one side of 4 bread slices in egg mixture for 10 seconds. Heat a small frying pan sprayed with nonstick cooking spray to medium heat. Place soaked side of bread down in pan. Spread one-fourth of the cream cheese mixture on top and then lightly press banana slices over cream cheese mixture. Soak one side of another bread slice and then place dry side down over bananas; press slightly with a wide spatula to seal. Repeat to make more "sandwiches." Cover and cook for 1 to 2 minutes on each side, or until lightly browned. Serve warm with a drizzle of caramel or other syrup, if desired. Makes 4 servings.

German Style

Try this French toast version of the classic German oven pancake for something unique and flavorful.

3 large eggs, separated

1 cup milk

1/4 cup frozen lemonade
   concentrate, thawed

Zest of 1 lemon

1 teaspoon vanilla

1/2 teaspoon salt

2 cups toasted unseasoned
   breadcrumbs

8 (1-inch-thick) slices day-old
   French bread

4 to 6 Granny Smith apples, cored,
   peeled and thinly sliced

2 tablespoons butter

1 jar (8 ounces) caramel sauce

8 tablespoons cinnamon sugar

In a pie pan or other shallow pan, whisk together the egg yolks, milk, lemonade concentrate, lemon zest, vanilla and salt. Whisk the egg whites and then place in a separate pie pan. Spread breadcrumbs on a plate. Dip both sides of each bread slice first in egg mixture, then in egg whites and then in breadcrumbs. Place coated bread on a baking sheet that has been sprayed with nonstick cooking spray. Bake at 350 degrees for 15 minutes; turn over and bake 15 minutes more. Meanwhile, sauté apple slices over medium-high heat in butter until cooked through and lightly browned, about 10 minutes. Stir in caramel sauce and turn off heat. Remove bread slices from oven and sprinkle with cinnamon sugar. Top with apple mixture and serve immediately. Makes 8 slices.

Huevos Rancheros Stacks

This South-of-the-Border breakfast is even better with a base of tortilla French toast. Olé!

3 large eggs

1 cup milk

1 teaspoon chipotle chile powder

1/2 teaspoon salt

12 small (6-inch diameter)
*   flour tortillas*

1 can (16 ounces) refried beans

3 cups grated cheddar cheese

1 can (14 ounces)
*   red enchilada sauce*

6 poached or fried eggs

In a pie pan or other shallow pan, whisk together the eggs, milk, chile powder and salt. Dip a tortilla in egg mixture and then cook for 30 seconds on each side in a frying pan sprayed with nonstick cooking spray over medium-high heat. Spread another tablespoon egg mixture on cooked side of tortilla and then flip and cook 30 seconds more; continue this process with each tortilla until a layer of lightly browned egg mixture coats each side. Place a tortilla on a microwaveable serving plate and spread with 3 tablespoons refried beans. Sprinkle 1/4 cup cheese over beans. Place another tortilla over beans and pour 1/4 cup enchilada sauce over top, allowing sauce to drizzle over the edges. Place an egg on the sauce and then drizzle with a little more sauce and sprinkle with 1/4 cup cheese. Microwave for 1 minute, or until cheese is melted and stack is heated through. Makes 6 servings.

Apple Nut Stuffed

THIS IS A SURE WINNER FOR AN EASY AND DELICIOUS FRUIT-AND-NUT-STUFFED BREAKFAST TREAT.

8 ounces cream cheese, softened

2 tablespoons powdered sugar

1/2 teaspoon cinnamon

1 can (21 ounces) apple pie filling

1 teaspoon orange zest

1/2 cup diced pecans or walnuts

1/4 cup diced raisins or
    dried cranberries

2 eggs

1/2 cup milk

1/4 cup unsweetened applesauce

8 (1 1/2-inch-thick) slices day-old
    French bread

Using a hand mixer, mix together the cream cheese, sugar and cinnamon in a bowl. In another bowl, stir together the apple pie filling, orange zest, nuts and raisins. In a pie pan or other shallow pan, whisk together the eggs, milk and applesauce. Slice bread slices almost in half and then lay out flat, butterfly style. Spread each side of bread with 1 tablespoon cream cheese mixture. Spread 1/4 cup apple mixture in center and then close bread, pressing slightly with a wide spatula to seal. Dip both sides of bread in egg mixture. Heat a small frying pan sprayed with nonstick cooking spray to medium heat. Cover and cook soaked bread for 2 to 3 minutes on each side, or until lightly browned. Makes 8 servings.

Raspberry Cheesecake

THE CREAMY RASPBERRY CENTER IS SO DELICIOUS YOU WILL WONDER IF THIS IS BREAKFAST OR DESSERT!

3 large eggs

1 cup milk

1 teaspoon vanilla

1/2 teaspoon salt

12 (1/2-inch-thick) slices day-old French bread

8 ounces cheesecake-flavored whipped cream cheese*

6 tablespoons low-sugar raspberry jam

Raspberry Syrup (see page 121)

*If cheesecake-flavored cream cheese is not available, use 8 ounces regular whipped cream cheese and stir in 2 tablespoons instant cheesecake pudding mix.

In a pie pan or shallow pan, whisk together the eggs, milk, vanilla and salt. Spread one side of 6 bread slices with 1 tablespoon cream cheese. Spread 1 tablespoon jam on one side of the remaining slices. Put the slices together to form sandwiches, pressing slightly with a wide spatula to seal. Dip both sides of sandwiches in egg mixture. Heat a small frying pan sprayed with nonstick cooking spray to medium heat. Cover and cook sandwiches for 2 to 3 minutes on each side, or until lightly browned. Serve with Raspberry Syrup. Makes 6 servings.

Special Occasion

New Year's Brunch Shrimp Bites

THESE SEAFOOD APPETIZERS WILL ADD A GOURMET TOUCH TO YOUR NEW YEAR'S FEAST.

12 slices day-old dark
pumpernickel bread
1 cup milk
2 tablespoons flour
1/2 teaspoon salt
3 large eggs
Butter
1/2 cup whipped cream cheese
3 tablespoons basil and
pine nut pesto
24 jumbo cooked-and-peeled
deli shrimp, chilled

With a cookie cutter approximately 2 1/2 to 3 inches in diameter (festive shapes preferred!), cut 2 shapes from each slice of bread, making 24 pieces total. In a pie pan or other shallow pan, whisk together the milk, flour and salt; whisk in eggs until well blended. Dip bread pieces in egg mixture for a few seconds on each side and wipe away any excess. Melt a little butter in a small frying pan over medium-high heat. Cover and cook soaked bread a few pieces at a time about 2 to 3 minutes on each side, or until well browned and crisp. Place on wire cookie racks and cool to room temperature. Mix together cream cheese and pesto. Place a rounded teaspoonful of cream cheese mixture on each bread piece, making sure to use all the cream cheese mixture. Set a shrimp, thickest side down and tail in the air, on top; serve chilled. Makes 24 appetizers.

Cherry Valentines

WAKE YOUR VALENTINE WITH A SWEET AND CREAMY ROMANTIC BREAKFAST.

1 cup heavy cream, whipped

1/4 cup sugar

1 teaspoon vanilla

8 ounces whipped cream cheese

1 cup milk

3 large eggs

1 teaspoon almond extract

1/2 teaspoon salt

Few drops red food coloring,
     if desired

8 slices day-old firm white bread

Chunky Cherry Syrup (see
     page 123)

Using a hand mixer, mix together the whipped cream, sugar, vanilla and cream cheese in a bowl; chill. In a pie pan or other shallow pan, whisk together the milk, eggs, almond extract and salt. Add a few drops of red food coloring to make mixture pink, if desired. Cut bread slices into large heart shapes with a heart-shaped cookie cutter. Soak bread slices in egg mixture for 10 seconds on each side. Heat a frying pan sprayed with nonstick spray over medium heat. Cover and cook soaked bread in the pan 2 to 3 minutes on each side, or until lightly browned. Let each slice cool to room temperature. Place one-fourth of the chilled cream filling between two French toast slices. Ladle generously with Chunky Cherry Syrup and serve sprinkled with powdered sugar as a garnish. Makes 4 servings.

Red, White and Blueberry Stacks

TOP YOUR PATRIOTIC BREAKFAST STACK WITH A LITTLE FLAG TO MAKE IT EXTRA SPECIAL!

1 1/2 cups heavy cream, whipped

1/4 cup sugar

1 teaspoon vanilla

8 ounces whipped cream cheese

1 1/2 cups milk

4 large eggs

1 teaspoon vanilla

1/2 teaspoon salt

16 slices day-old firm white bread

8 cups blueberries

8 cups diced strawberries

Chunky Cherry Syrup (see page 123) or Raspberry Syrup (see page 121)

Using a hand mixer, mix together the whipped cream, sugar, vanilla and cream cheese in a bowl; chill. In a pie pan or other shallow pan, whisk together the milk, eggs, vanilla and salt. Cut each bread slice with a large star-shaped cookie cutter. Soak the stars in egg mixture for 10 seconds on each side. Heat a frying pan sprayed with nonstick cooking spray over medium heat. Cover and cook soaked bread for 2 to 3 minutes on each side, or until well browned. Let each slice cool to room temperature. Place 1/4 cup of the chilled cream filling on 8 French toast slices. Sprinkle 1/2 cup blueberries and 1/2 cup strawberries over cream filling. Set remaining French toast slices on top. Ladle generously with Chunky Cherry or Raspberry Syrup and then garnish with another dollop of cream filling. Makes 8 servings.

Harvest Pumpkin Spice

WARM UP ON A CRISP FALL DAY WITH THIS SPECIAL TREAT MADE WITH
CINNAMON, NUTMEG, CREAM AND PUMPKIN BREAD.

1 cup heavy cream, whipped
1/4 cup sugar
1 teaspoon vanilla
8 ounces whipped cream cheese
1 teaspoon cinnamon
1/2 teaspoon nutmeg
3 large eggs
1 cup milk
1/2 teaspoon salt
8 (1/2-inch-thick) slices sturdy,
 day-old pumpkin bread

Using a hand mixer, mix together the whipped cream, sugar, vanilla, cream cheese and spices in a bowl; chill. In a pie pan or other shallow pan, whisk together the eggs, milk and salt. Soak bread slices in egg mixture for about 30 seconds on each side. Heat a small frying pan sprayed with nonstick spray to medium heat. Place soaked bread in pan and cover and cook for 2 to 3 minutes on each side, or until lightly browned. Remove and let cool to slightly warm. Place a bread slice on a plate and then spread a thick layer of cream cheese mixture on top. Garnish with a little sprinkle of nutmeg or cinnamon, if desired. Makes 8 slices.

Fondue Party

You'll forget about boring cubes of angel food cake once you start dipping warm cubes of French toast into sweet syrups, delectable cookie crumbs and fresh fruit.

2 cups milk

1/2 cup flour

6 large eggs

1 tablespoon vanilla

1 teaspoon salt

1 loaf day-old French bread

Butter

Diced fresh fruits, nuts
and coconut

Crumbled sugar cookies or
other favorite cookies

1 or 2 specialty syrups
(see pages 120–126)

In a pie pan or other shallow pan, whisk together the milk and flour; whisk in eggs, vanilla and salt. Cut bread into 2-inch cubes, with crust on one side of each chunk. Soak bread chunks in egg mixture for 10 to 20 seconds on each side, or until just soaked through. Heat a little butter in a small frying pan over medium-high heat. Cook soaked bread in the pan 1 to 2 minutes on all sides, or until lightly browned. Place cooked bread cubes on a baking tray in a warm oven to keep warm until served. Place fruits, nuts, coconut and cookie crumbs on individual serving plates. Pour syrup into a fondue pot and serve warm bread cubes on a serving platter. Pierce bread cubes with toothpicks or skewers, crust side first, and dip in syrup and then in favorite toppings. Makes 6 to 8 servings.

Christmas Morning Casserole

BEGIN A DELICIOUS NEW HOLIDAY TRADITION WITH EGGNOG FRENCH TOAST. DON'T FORGET TO INVITE SANTA!

2 1/2 cups eggnog
3 large eggs
1 teaspoon nutmeg
1 teaspoon cinnamon
1/2 teaspoon salt
1 large loaf French bread
Cranapple Compote (see page 123)

In a bowl, whisk together the eggnog, eggs, nutmeg, cinnamon and salt. Pour half of the eggnog mixture into a 9 x 13-inch baking pan. Cut ends off bread and discard. Slice bread into 8 slices, each about 1 1/2 inches thick, and then place in pan. Pour remaining eggnog mixture over slices and cover and refrigerate overnight. Remove from refrigerator and turn each slice over in pan with a wide spatula; bring to room temperature, about 30 minutes. Bake at 425 degrees for 20 minutes. Carefully turn slices over with a wide spatula and bake 10 to 15 minutes more, or until puffed and browned. Serve with Cranapple Compote. Makes 6 to 8 servings.

Casseroles

French Twist Casserole

THE ELEGANTLY SPIRALED CROISSANTS COMBINED WITH MAPLE CREAM MAKE
THIS A SINFULLY RICH CASSEROLE.

Maple Cream Syrup (see page 120)
6 large (6-inch) day-old croissants
3 large eggs
1 cup milk
1/2 teaspoon salt
1 teaspoon vanilla

Spray a 2 1/2-quart-round baking dish generously with nonstick cooking spray. Pour half of
the Maple Cream Syrup into bottom of the
pan. Tear croissants in half width-wise (through
the wide middle) so that each piece has a
curved, horn-shaped end. Overlap croissants
around side of pan like a fan, with the pointed
ends facing down in the center of the pan.
Pour remaining syrup over croissants. In a bowl,
whisk together the eggs, milk, salt and vanilla
and then pour over top. Cover and refrigerate
a few hours or overnight. Remove from refrigerator and let come to room temperature,
about 30 minutes. Bake, uncovered, at 350
degrees for 45 to 50 minutes, or until browned
and liquid is absorbed. Makes 4 to 6 servings.

Triple Strawberries and Cream

THIS SWEET CLASSIC COMBINATION WILL BECOME THE DISH THAT EVERYONE BEGS YOU TO MAKE.

12 (1-inch-thick) slices day-old
   French bread
6 ounces light cream cheese
1/2 cup low-sugar strawberry jam
4 large eggs
2 cups milk
2 tablespoons sugar
1 teaspoon salt
2 cups sliced fresh strawberries
1 cup strawberry syrup
Whipped cream or topping

Remove crusts from bread. Spread one side of 6 bread slices with 1 tablespoon cream cheese. Equally divide and spread jam on one side of remaining bread slices. Lightly press cream cheese and jam slices together to seal. Place sandwiches in a greased 9 x 13-inch baking pan, completely filling pan. In a bowl, whisk together the eggs, milk, sugar and salt. Pour half of the egg mixture over sandwiches. Cover and refrigerate at least 2 hours or overnight. Remove from refrigerator and carefully turn sandwiches over; pour remaining egg mixture over top. Bring to room temperature, about 30 minutes. Bake, uncovered, at 350 degrees for 35 to 40 minutes, or until golden brown. Cut into squares and serve with sliced strawberries, syrup, and a dollop of whipped cream. Makes 6 servings.

Pecan Praline

THE SOOTHING SPICES AND SUBTLE NUTTINESS OF THIS DISH WILL FILL YOUR TUMMY WITH GOODNESS.

1 loaf day-old French bread

6 large eggs

1/4 teaspoon nutmeg

1/2 teaspoon cinnamon

1/2 teaspoon salt

1 tablespoon vanilla

3 cups milk

1/4 cup butter

2 tablespoons corn syrup

1 cup light brown sugar

1 cup chopped pecans

Spray a 9 x 13-inch baking pan with nonstick cooking spray. Slice bread into eight 1 1/2-inch slices and then lay in pan, filling pan completely. In a bowl, whisk together the eggs, spices, salt, vanilla and milk. Pour egg mixture over bread slices in pan and then cover and refrigerate overnight. Remove from refrigerator and turn each slice over in pan with a wide spatula; bring to room temperature, about 30 minutes. In a bowl, combine the butter, corn syrup, brown sugar and pecans. Sprinkle mixture over bread slices. Bake, uncovered, at 350 degrees for 50 minutes. Remove from oven and let stand 10 minutes before serving. Makes 6 to 8 servings.

Streusel Topped

This coffee cake–style breakfast casserole will wake even the soundest of sleepers.

4 eggs
2 cups milk
1 teaspoon cinnamon
1/2 teaspoon salt
4 tablespoons vanilla
1/3 cup sugar
1 large loaf day-old French bread

Streusel Topping:
1/3 cup brown sugar
1/4 cup butter
1 tablespoon flour
1/3 cup quick oats
1/2 teaspoon cinnamon
1/4 cup chopped pecans

In a bowl, whisk together the eggs, milk, cinnamon, salt, vanilla and sugar. Pour half of the mixture into a 9 x 13-inch pan sprayed with nonstick cooking spray. Cut bread into slices 1 1/2 inches thick and then lay in pan, filling completely. Pour remaining egg mixture over top and then cover and refrigerate overnight. Remove from refrigerator and bring to room temperature, about 30 minutes. Bake, uncovered, at 450 degrees for 15 minutes.

Mix topping ingredients together and then sprinkle over casserole and bake 10 minutes more. Makes 6 to 8 servings.

Pineapple Upside Down

FORGET THE ORIGINAL CAKE VERSION OF THIS CLASSIC RECIPE—FRENCH TOAST IS THE PERFECT VEHICLE FOR THIS PINEAPPLE TREAT.

1/4 cup butter

1/2 cup brown sugar

2 tablespoons corn syrup

1 can (20 ounces) pineapple rings,
    1/4 cup juice reserved

6 maraschino cherries

6 slices day-old Texas-style
    toast (or thickly sliced,
    firm white bread)

3 large eggs

1 cup milk

1/2 teaspoon salt

1/2 teaspoon cinnamon

1 teaspoon vanilla

In a small frying pan, simmer butter, brown sugar and corn syrup until sugar is dissolved. Pour mixture into a 9 x 13-inch baking pan sprayed with nonstick spray and spread evenly in pan. Place pineapple rings in pan, evenly spaced apart so each ring will be in the center of a bread slice when bread is placed on top. Place a cherry in the center of each ring. Place bread slices on top of pine-apple and cher-ries, pressing down slightly with a spatula so that rings are pressed into bread slices. In a bowl, whisk together eggs, milk, salt, cinnamon and vanilla and then pour over the bread slices, making sure each slice is saturated. Cover and refrigerate at least 2 hours or overnight. Remove from refrigerator and bring to room temperature, about 30 minutes. Bake, uncovered, at 375 degrees for 40 to 45 min-utes, or until puffed and lightly browned. Flip over onto a serving plate and serve inverted. Makes 6 servings.

Blueberries and Cream Soufflé

THIS DELICIOUS BERRY CASSEROLE COULD BECOME A TRUE BLUE FAVORITE.

2 packages (8 ounces each)
   Neufchâtel or light
   cream cheese
10 cups cubed day-old French
   bread (about 1-inch cubes)
2 cups fresh or frozen blueberries
8 large eggs
2 cups whole milk
2 tablespoons sugar
1/2 cup pure maple syrup
Blueberry Syrup (see page 121)

Spray a 3 1/2- to 4-quart casserole generously with nonstick cooking spray. Cut one of the cream cheese packages into small cubes. Toss together the cream cheese cubes, bread cubes and blueberries and then place mixture in the casserole dish. Soften the remaining cream cheese in the microwave for 60 seconds. In a bowl, whisk together the softened cream cheese, eggs, milk, sugar and maple syrup. Pour mixture evenly over bread mixture. Cover and refrigerate 2 hours or overnight. Remove from refrigerator and bring to room temperature, about 30 minutes. Bake, uncovered, at 375 degrees for 50 to 60 minutes, or until lightly browned and set in the center. Serve with Blueberry Syrup and sprinkle with powdered sugar, if desired. Makes 6 to 8 servings.

Variation: *Once mixture is ready to bake, it can be scooped into individual ramekins and baked about 30 to 35 minutes, or until lightly browned and set in the center.*

Sticky Buns

TRY THIS GOOEY CINNAMON FRENCH TOAST TO SATISFY YOUR CRAVING FOR CINNAMON ROLLS—AN EASY CROWD PLEASER.

1/2 cup butter

1 cup brown sugar

3 tablespoons corn syrup

1/2 cup diced pecans

8 (1-inch-thick) slices day-old
   French bread

6 large eggs

1 1/2 cups milk

1 teaspoon vanilla

1 teaspoon cinnamon

1/2 teaspoon salt

In a small saucepan over medium-high heat, melt butter and brown sugar until sugar is dissolved, stirring constantly; add corn syrup and cook until thickened, about 2 to 3 minutes. Pour mixture into a 9 x 13-inch baking pan sprayed with nonstick spray and sprinkle nuts over top. Place bread slices over nuts, completely filling pan and forming a single layer. In a bowl, whisk together the eggs, milk, vanilla, cinnamon and salt and then pour over bread slices, saturating evenly. Cover and refrigerate 2 hours or overnight. Remove from refrigerator and bring to room temperature, about 30 minutes. Bake, uncovered, at 350 degrees for 45 to 50 minutes, or until lightly browned. Let stand 10 minutes before serving inverted on serving plates. Makes 6 to 8 servings.

Rise 'n' Shine Breakfast Soufflé

THIS SAVORY BREAKFAST DISH IS THE PERFECT COMBINATION OF EGGS, BACON AND CHEESE.

1 loaf day-old French bread, cubed
    (about 8 cups)
8 ounces sharp cheddar
    cheese, grated
1/2 cup diced fresh flat-leaf parsley
8 large eggs
4 cups milk
1 teaspoon dry mustard
1 teaspoon seasoned salt
1/2 teaspoon white pepper
1/2 cup diced tomatoes
1/2 cup diced cooked bacon

Generously spray a 4-quart baking dish with nonstick cooking spray. Toss bread cubes with half of the cheese and then place mixture in baking dish. Sprinkle remaining cheese and parsley over top. In a bowl, whisk together the eggs, milk and spices. Pour egg mixture over bread and cheese. Sprinkle tomatoes and bacon on top and then cover and refrigerate overnight. Remove from refrigerator and bring to room temperature, about 30 minutes. Bake, uncovered, at 375 degrees for 45 to 50 minutes, or until puffed and lightly browned. Makes 4 to 6 servings.

Hazelnut Breakfast Ring

THIS DELICIOUS BREAKFAST DELIGHT IS INCREDIBLY EASY AND LOOKS GORGEOUS ON A SERVING PLATTER IN THE CENTER OF THE TABLE.

4 large eggs
1 bottle (16 ounces) liquid hazelnut coffee creamer
1/2 cup milk
1/2 teaspoon nutmeg
12 cups cubed day-old French bread (about 1-inch cubes)
1 cup diced hazelnuts
1 cup dark brown sugar
1 teaspoon cinnamon

In a bowl, whisk together the eggs, creamer, milk and nutmeg. Toss bread cubes in egg mixture and let stand about 3 minutes, tossing a few times to make sure all liquid is absorbed evenly. Generously spray a 2 1/2-quart nonstick bundt pan with nonstick cooking spray. Mix together nuts, brown sugar and cinnamon. Sprinkle about half of the nut mixture in the bottom of th pan. Spread 1/2 cup soaked bread cubes in pan, pressing down with a large spoon to remove air pockets. Sprinkle remaining nut mixture over top. Spread remaining bread cubes over nut mixture, pressing down to remove air pockets. Bake at 375 degrees for 35 to 40 minutes, or until firm. Flip pan over and invert casserole onto a serving platter. Serve warm with syrup if desired. Makes 8 to 10 servings.

Shrimp Croissant Casserole

AN EASY YET ELEGANT CASSEROLE FILLED WITH THE SAVORY TASTES OF SHRIMP, CHEESE AND ONION.

4 large day-old croissants

8 ounces Monterey Jack or
    Havarti cheese, grated

8 ounces cooked tiny
    cocktail shrimp

3 green onions, thinly sliced

4 large eggs

1 1/2 cups milk

1/2 teaspoon salt

1/2 teaspoon white pepper

Tear (do not cut) croissants into 1-inch pieces. Spray an 8 x 11-inch baking pan with nonstick cooking spray and then spread half of the croissant pieces in the pan. Spread half of the cheese, and all of the shrimp and green onions on top. Spread remaining croissant pieces on top and then sprinkle with remaining cheese. In a bowl, whisk together the eggs, milk, salt and pepper and then pour over top. Cover and refrigerate for several hours or overnight. Remove from refrigerator and bring to room temperature, about 30 minutes. Bake, uncovered, at 350 degrees for 40 to 45 minutes, or until firm. Let stand for 10 minutes before serving. Makes 4 servings.

Nutty Cinnamon Raisin Breakfast

THIS DISH HAS JUST THE RIGHT MEDLEY OF CRUNCHY, CREAMY AND FRUITY—
A LITTLE SOMETHING TO PLEASE EVERYONE.

1 loaf (16 ounces) day-old
   cinnamon raisin bread
1/2 cup diced pecans
1 can (20 ounces) crushed
   pineapple, with juice
1/4 cup butter, melted
4 large eggs
1/2 cup sugar
1/2 cup milk
1/2 teaspoon salt

Cut the bread into 1-inch pieces. Toss bread with nuts and pineapple with juice. Spread bread mixture in an 8 x 11-inch baking pan sprayed with nonstick cooking spray. In a bowl, whisk together the remaining ingredients and then pour over bread mixture, making sure the bread is saturated; let stand 20 minutes. Bake, uncovered, at 375 degrees for 35 to 40 minutes, or until firm and lightly browned. Serve cut into squares and sprinkled with powdered sugar or drizzled with syrup if desired. Makes 4 to 6 servings.

Crab Strata Supreme

YOU'LL ENJOY DELICIOUS LAYERS OF CRAB, ONION, MUSHROOMS, CHEESE AND MORE IN THIS FLAVORFUL CASSEROLE.

2 tablespoons butter
1 red bell pepper, diced
3 green onions, thinly sliced
8 ounces mushrooms, diced
2 cups diced celery
10 cups cubed day-old French bread
    (about 1-inch cubes)
8 ounces crabmeat, diced
2 cups grated Swiss or
    Havarti cheese
8 large eggs
2 cups milk
1 cup sour cream
1/4 cup dry white wine or
    white grape juice
1 teaspoon dry mustard
1/2 teaspoon each salt and
    white pepper
1/2 cup grated Parmesan cheese

In a frying pan over medium-high heat, sauté butter, bell pepper, onion, mushrooms and celery until onion is translucent, about 3 minutes. Toss sautéed mixture in a large bowl with the bread cubes. Spread mixture into a 3 1/2- to 4-quart casserole that has been sprayed with nonstick cooking spray. Spread crab and then cheese on top. In a bowl, whisk together all remaining ingredients except the Parmesan cheese; pour over crab. Cover and refrigerate several hours or overnight. Remove from refrigerator and bring to room temperature, about 30 minutes. Bake, covered, at 350 degrees for 30 minutes. Remove cover and sprinkle Parmesan cheese over casserole. Bake, uncovered, 15 minutes more. Let stand for 10 minutes before serving. Makes 6 to 8 servings.

Peach Melba Casserole

A GREAT NEW TWIST ON THE TRADITIONAL PEACH AND RASPBERRY DESSERT AS A BREAKFAST TREAT.

4 large eggs, divided
2 cups half-and-half
1/2 cup sugar
1 teaspoon vanilla
1/2 teaspoon salt
Few dashes nutmeg
12 to 14 slices day-old firm white
  bread, crusts removed
8 ounces cream cheese, softened
3 tablespoons peach jam
2 large ripe peaches, peeled
  and thinly sliced
Raspberry Syrup (see page 121)

In a bowl, whisk together 3 eggs, half-and-half, sugar, vanilla, salt and nutmeg. Pour half of the egg mixture into a 9 x 13-inch pan. Arrange half of the bread slices in the pan, completely covering bottom of pan. In a bowl, mix together with a fork cream cheese, 1 egg and jam and then spread over bread slices. Spread peach slices on top in a single layer. Place remaining bread slices on top of peaches, completely covering surface. Pour remaining egg mixture over top, making sure to saturate evenly. Cover and refrigerate 2 hours or overnight. Remove from refrigerator and bring to room temperature, about 30 minutes. Bake at 350 degrees for 30 to 40 minutes, or until golden brown on top. Serve hot with Raspberry Syrup. Makes 4 to 6 servings.

Ciabatta, Gruyère and Sausage

THE CRUSTY BREAD, CHEESE AND SAUSAGE MAKE THIS CASSEROLE A DELIGHTFUL COMBINATION OF FLAVORS AND TEXTURES.

8 ounces large turkey or chicken sausages (casings removed)
1 loaf (16 ounces) day-old ciabatta or panini
1/2 cup thinly sliced green onions
1/2 cup diced fresh flat-leaf parsley
8 ounces Gruyère cheese, grated
2 1/2 cups milk
6 large eggs
1/2 teaspoon salt

Crumble sausages into a heated frying pan. Cook over high heat until lightly browned; remove from heat. Cut bread into 1-inch cubes and then toss with cooked sausage, onions, parsley and cheese in a large bowl. Spray a 9 x 13-inch pan with nonstick cooking spray and then spread bread mixture in pan. In a bowl, whisk together the milk, eggs and salt and then pour over top, saturating bread evenly. Cover and refrigerate 2 hours or overnight. Remove from refrigerator and bring to room temperature, about 30 minutes. Bake, uncovered, at 350 degrees for 45 to 50 minutes, or until cooked through and lightly browned on top. Makes 6 to 8 servings.

Caramelized Pear

THIS BREAKFAST DELIGHT WILL WAKE UP THE HOUSEHOLD WITH ITS TEMPTING PEAR AND CINNAMON COMBINATION.

4 tablespoons butter

2 large Bosc pears, peeled and sliced 1/4 inch thick

1 cup light brown sugar

4 tablespoons light corn syrup

1 loaf challah or French bread, sliced 1 inch thick

6 eggs

2 cups milk

1 teaspoon cinnamon

1/4 teaspoon nutmeg

1 teaspoon vanilla

1/2 teaspoon salt

Melt butter in a medium frying pan and then sauté pear slices for 2 to 3 minutes over high heat, or until lightly browned, stirring constantly to release moisture from pears. Remove pear slices and spread in a 9 x 13-inch pan. Add brown sugar and corn syrup to the frying pan and then heat to a simmer. Cook 1 to 2 minutes, or until sugar is dissolved. Pour sugar mixture over pear slices. Lay bread slices on top, completely filling pan. In a bowl, whisk together remaining ingredients and then pour over bread slices, saturating evenly. Cover and refrigerate 2 hours or overnight. Remove from refrigerator and bring to room temperature, about 30 minutes. Bake, uncovered, at 350 degrees for 45 to 50 minutes, or until cooked through and lightly browned on top. Makes 6 to 8 servings.

Savory Entrées

Southwest Chile and Cheese

THE BLEND OF CHILES AND CHEESE WILL MAKE THIS CASSEROLE A NEW FAMILY FAVORITE.

3 Anaheim chiles

1 jalapeño

8 cups cubed day-old French
   bread (about 1-inch cubes)

8 ounces sharp cheddar
   cheese, grated

4 ounces sharp white cheddar or
   Monterey Jack cheese, grated

1/2 cup thinly sliced green onion

1/2 cup chopped fresh cilantro

6 large eggs

2 cups milk

1 tablespoon cumin

1 teaspoon chipotle chile powder

1 teaspoon salt

Slice chiles and jalapeño in half lengthwise and remove seeds and pulp. Grill or broil, cut sides facing away from the heat, for 3 to 5 minutes, or until skin is blackened. Place in a ziplock bag and allow to sweat for 5 minutes. Remove skins and dice chiles and jalapeño. Toss bread cubes with chiles, cheeses, onion and cilantro. Place in a 4-quart casserole that has been sprayed with nonstick cooking spray. Mix remaining ingredients together and then pour over bread mixture, making sure all the bread cubes are saturated. Bake, uncovered, at 375 degrees for 35 to 40 minutes, or until lightly browned and almost set in the center. Makes 4 to 6 servings.

French Toast Chili Stacks

WITH THAT SPICY CHIPOTLE TASTE, THIS RECIPE WILL SOON BECOME A NEW SOUTHWEST FAVORITE!

1 large egg
1 cup milk
1/4 cup flour
1/2 teaspoon salt
2 teaspoons chipotle chile powder
4 day-old flatbread or soft pita
   bread rounds (7-inch diameter)
Butter
4 cups chili, any kind
2 cups grated cheddar cheese
Diced lettuce, tomato and onion

In a pie pan or other shallow pan, whisk together the egg, milk, flour, salt and chile powder. Soak flatbread or pitas rounds one at a time in egg mixture for 3 to 5 minutes on each side, or until soaked through and softened. (The softer the flatbread or pitas, the less soaking time is needed.) Heat a little butter in an 8-inch frying pan. Cover and cook soaked flatbread or pita rounds one at a time in pan over medium-high heat for 2 to 3 minutes on each side, or until well browned. Heat chili in microwave oven. Place one cooked flatbread or pita round on a microwave-safe plate. Spread 1 cup chili over top. Top with 1/2 cup grated cheese and then microwave for 30 to 60 seconds, or until bubbly around edges. Remove and top with lettuce, tomato and onion, if desired. Makes 4 servings.

Tomato Basil Monte Cristos

THIS UPDATE OF THE CLASSIC SANDWICH WILL TURN LUNCH INTO A TASTE OF FRANCE!

1/2 cup flour
1 1/2 cups seasoned toasted
    breadcrumbs
4 eggs
1/2 cup milk
4 (1/4-inch-thick) slices
    mozzarella cheese
8 slices day-old firm white bread
1 large vine-ripened tomato,
    thinly sliced
1 bunch fresh basil, diced

Spread flour and breadcrumbs on separate plates. In a pie pan or other shallow pan, whisk together the eggs and milk. Place 1 slice cheese on 4 bread slices. Spread tomato slices and a little basil on the remaining bread slices. Press the slices together, with tomatoes, basil and cheese in the middle. Dip the outsides of the sandwich in the following order: flour, egg mixture and then breadcrumbs. Place in small frying pan sprayed with nonstick cooking spray over medium heat. Cover and cook about 2 minutes on each side, or until golden brown. Makes 4 servings.

Southwest Monte Cristos

HAM, TURKEY AND CHEESE WITH A LITTLE KICK OF JALAPEÑO IS THE PERFECT COMBINATION FOR THIS SAVORY SANDWICH.

1/2 cup flour
1 1/2 cups seasoned toasted
breadcrumbs
4 eggs
1/2 cup milk
4 tablespoons jalapeño jelly
8 slices day-old firm white bread
4 (1/4-inch-thick) slices
pepper jack cheese
8 tablespoons thinly sliced
green onions
4 slices deli ham
4 slices deli smoked turkey

Spread flour and breadcrumbs on separate plates. In a pie pan or other shallow pan, whisk together the eggs and milk. Spread 1 tablespoon jelly on 4 bread slices. Sprinkle 1 tablespoon green onion over jelly. Place a slice cheese on the remaining bread slices. Place a slice of ham and turkey over cheese; press two slices together, with jelly, meat and cheese in the middle. Dip the outsides of the sandwich in the following order: flour, egg mixture and then breadcrumbs. Place in small frying pan sprayed with nonstick cooking spray over medium heat. Cover and cook 2 minutes on each side, or until golden brown. Makes 4 servings.

Ham and Swiss Monte Cristos

DRESS UP THE USUAL HAM AND CHEESE SANDWICH WITH CARAMELIZED ONIONS AND TOASTED BREADCRUMBS.

1/2 cup flour

1 1/2 cups seasoned toasted
   breadcrumbs

4 eggs

1/2 cup milk

1 large Vidalia or yellow
   onion, julienned

2 tablespoons butter

1/4 teaspoon nutmeg, optional

8 slices baby Swiss or
   Havarti cheese

8 slices day-old firm white bread

4 slices deli ham

Spread flour and breadcrumbs on separate plates. In a pie pan or other shallow pan, whisk together the eggs and milk. Sauté onion over medium-high heat in butter, stirring often, until caramelized and lightly browned; stir in nutmeg, if desired. Place 1 slice cheese on each bread slice. Spread 1/2 cup onion mixture over 4 of the bread slices with cheese. Place 1 slice ham over onions. Press the slices together, with cheese slices, ham and onions in the middle. Dip the outsides of the sandwich in the following order: flour, egg mixture and then breadcrumbs. Place in small frying pan sprayed with nonstick cooking spray over medium heat. Cover and cook about 2 minutes on each side, or until golden brown. Makes 4 servings.

French Onion Baked Monte Cristos

THIS CLASSIC SANDWICH WITH THAT GREAT ONION TASTE BAKED RIGHT INTO THE BREAD IS ONE YOUR WHOLE FAMILY WILL LOVE.

4 large eggs

1 cup milk

1 envelope dry French onion
   soup mix

8 slices day-old firm white bread

8 slices Swiss cheese

4 slices deli ham

4 slices deli turkey

1/2 cup sour cream

2 tablespoons Dijon mustard

In a pie pan or other shallow pan, whisk together the eggs, milk and soup mix. Soak one side of 4 bread slices in egg mixture for about 30 seconds. Place soaked side down in a 9 x 13-inch-baking pan sprayed with nonstick cooking spray. Layer a slice of cheese, a slice of ham, a slice of turkey and another slice of cheese on top of the dry side of each bread slice. Soak one side of remaining bread slices in egg mixture for 30 seconds. Place dry side down on top of cheese slices to make sandwiches. Bake at 425 degrees for 5 minutes. Remove from oven and carefully turn each sandwich over. Return to oven and bake 5 minutes more. Turn oven to broil for 1 minute; turn off oven and let sandwiches sit inside a few minutes more. In a small bowl, mix together the sour cream and mustard. Serve sandwiches hot with sour cream mixture drizzled over top or on the side. Makes 4 servings.

Tuscan Supper Strata

A TASTE OF ITALY IS ONLY MINUTES AWAY WITH THIS COMBINATION OF PROSCIUTTO, MOZZARELLA, PARMESAN, BASIL AND TOMATO.

8 cups cubed day-old French
    bread (1-inch cubes)
8 ounces fresh mozzarella,
    cut into tiny cubes
8 ounces thinly sliced
    prosciutto, diced
3 large ripe tomatoes, diced
5 large eggs
1 1/2 cups milk
1/2 cup sour cream
1 teaspoon Italian seasonings
1 teaspoon dried basil
1/2 teaspoon each salt and
    garlic powder
1/2 cup grated Parmesan cheese

Toss bread cubes, cheese, prosciutto and tomatoes together in a large bowl. Spray a 9 x 13-inch baking pan with nonstick cooking spray and then spread bread mixture in pan. In a bowl, whisk together the remaining ingredients and then pour over bread mixture, making sure every bread cube is saturated. Cover and refrigerate 2 hours or overnight. Remove from refrigerator and bring to room temperature, about 30 minutes. Bake, uncovered, at 350 degrees for 40 to 45 minutes, or until firm and lightly browned. Sprinkle with Parmesan cheese, if desired. Makes 4 to 6 servings.

Savory Cheddar Crusted

THE CHEESE IN THIS RECIPE MAGICALLY COATS THE BREAD AND FORMS
A CRUNCHY GOLDEN BROWN CRUST.

2 large eggs

1 cup milk

1/2 cup sour cream

1/2 teaspoon salt

3 cups finely grated sharp
*   cheddar cheese*

1/2 cup grated Parmesan cheese

1 tablespoon flour

1 teaspoon garlic powder

1 tablespoon Italian seasonings

8 (1-inch-thick) slices day-old
*   French bread*

In a pie or other shallow pan, whisk together the eggs, milk, sour cream and salt until smooth. In a bowl, toss the cheeses with flour, garlic powder and Italian seasonings. Soak bread slices in egg mixture for about 60 seconds on each side. Heat a small nonstick frying pan sprayed with nonstick cooking spray to medium-high heat. Place a soaked bread slice in pan and cook, uncovered, about 2 minutes, or until lightly browned. Flip over with a wide spatula. Spread 2 tablespoons cheese mixture evenly on the cooked side of bread. After about 2 minutes, flip bread over again so that the cheese-covered side is facing down. Spread 2 tablespoons of cheese mixture evenly on side now facing up. After about 2 minutes, flip bread over. Cook another 1 to 2 minutes, or until the cheese on the other side is crisp and browned. Makes 8 slices.

Southwest
Chipotle Cornbread

TRY THIS FUN, FAST AND FLAVORFUL TWIST ON THE CLASSIC TAMALE PIE RECIPE.

3/4 cup cornmeal

1/4 cup flour

2 teaspoons chipotle chile powder

3 large eggs

1 cup milk

1/2 teaspoon salt

8 (1/2-inch-thick) slices sturdy
day-old cornbread

Canola oil

1 can (15 ounces) black beans,
drained and rinsed

1 can (12 ounces)
red enchilada sauce

6 ounces queso fresco, crumbled

1 tomato, diced

1 bunch fresh cilantro, diced

Mix together the cornmeal, flour and chile powder and then spread on a plate. In a pie pan or other shallow pan, whisk together the eggs, milk and salt. Dip cornbread slices first in egg mixture and then in cornmeal mixture. Heat a small frying pan with a little oil to medium heat. Cook in pan for 2 to 3 minutes on each side, or until browned. In a blender, mix together black beans and enchilada sauce and then heat in microwave about 90 seconds. Place a cooked cornbread slice on a plate and top with black bean sauce. Sprinkle with cheese, tomato and cilantro. Makes 8 servings.

Seafood
Newberg Stacks

THIS SNAPPY DINNER COMES TOGETHER EASY WITH LOBSTER BISQUE AND SHRIMP.

3 green onions, thinly sliced
1/2 green bell pepper, diced
1 tablespoon butter
1 can (14 ounces) lobster or
    shrimp bisque, condensed
1/2 pound cooked and
    peeled shrimp
1/2 pound cooked scallops
1/2 pound cooked regular
    or imitation crab
1 cup half-and-half
3 large eggs
1/2 teaspoon salt
6 day-old English muffins, split

In a large frying pan, sauté onions and bell pepper in butter over medium heat until limp but not browned; stir in condensed soup. Cut the seafood into uniform cubes, a little less than 1/2 inch. Add seafood to skillet and then cook until hot and bubbly around edges; keep warm. In a pie pan or other shallow pan, whisk together the half-and-half, eggs and salt. Dip English muffin halves in egg mixture for a few seconds on each side. Remove and let excess mixture drip off. Heat a small frying pan sprayed with nonstick cooking spray over medium heat. Cover and cook soaked muffins about 3 minutes on each side. Place a muffin half on a plate and top with 1/3 cup seafood mixture. Top with a second muffin half and 1/3 cup seafood mixture. Serve immediately. Makes 6 servings.

Savory Eggs in a Basket

Whip this up in 20 minutes and enjoy a savory meal that you can have for breakfast, lunch or even dinner!

8 large eggs, divided
1/2 cup milk
1/2 teaspoon garlic powder
1/2 teaspoon seasoned salt
6 slices day-old firm bread,
  crusts removed
1 cup grated cheddar cheese

Spray six 1-cup capacity muffin tins or ramekins generously with nonstick cooking spray. In a pie pan or other shallow pan, whisk together 2 eggs, milk, garlic powder and salt. Dip bread slices into egg mixture for 10 seconds on each side, and then press 1 soaked bread slice lightly into each muffin tin, forming a "basket" (corners of bread slices will be sticking out of muffin tin). Crack 1 egg into each of the baskets. Sprinkle a little cheese on top of each egg. Bake at 400 degrees for 15 minutes for eggs that will be slightly runny in the center, or cook longer for a more set egg yolk. Makes 6 servings.

French Toast Pizzas

THESE EASY AND FLAVORFUL INDIVIDUAL PIZZAS HAVE JUST THE RIGHT TASTE AND TEXTURE.

1 cup milk

1/4 cup flour

3 large eggs

1/2 teaspoon salt

Butter

6 slices day-old pita bread or
    flatbread (8-inch diameter)

3 cups pizza sauce

1 1/2 cups grated
    mozzarella cheese

Pizza toppings (such as pepperoni,
    olives, green peppers, onions)

1/2 cup grated Parmesan cheese

In a pie pan or other shallow pan, whisk together the milk and flour; whisk in eggs and salt. Soak each bread slice for 10 to 20 seconds on each side, or until just soaked through. Heat a little butter in a 9-inch frying pan over medium-high heat. Cook soaked bread in pan 1 to 2 minutes on each side, or until lightly browned. Place cooked pita rounds on a wire rack sprayed with nonstick cooking spray and set on a baking sheet. Bake at 400 degrees for 10 minutes. Remove from oven and spread 1/2 cup pizza sauce on each round. Sprinkle 1/4 cup mozzarella cheese over sauce and then spread any desired toppings over mozzarella. Turn oven to broil setting and then return pan to top rack in oven. Broil pizzas for a few minutes, watching closely so as not to burn. Remove from oven and sprinkle Parmesan cheese over top. Makes 6 servings.

30-Minute Skillet Strata

THIS QUICKER VERSION OF OVERNIGHT CASSEROLE IS EASY AND DELICIOUS!

6 large eggs

1 1/2 cups milk

1 cup grated sharp
    cheddar cheese

2 tablespoons dried parsley

1 teaspoon seasoned salt

1/4 cup butter

1 medium yellow onion, diced

1/2 cup cooked diced meat*

4 cups day-old firm
    white bread cubes

*Try cooked diced sausage, bacon, ham, smoked salmon or tiny cocktail shrimp.

In a bowl, whisk together the eggs, milk, cheese, parsley and salt. Melt butter in a 10-inch ovenproof frying pan and then cook onion over medium-high heat until translucent, about 3 minutes. Stir in meat and bread cubes and cook another 3 to 5 minutes, or until bread is coated and lightly toasted. Turn off heat and stir in egg mixture, mixing just until all bread cubes are soaked. Bake at 425 degrees for 16 to 18 minutes, or until puffed and browned on top. Makes 4 to 6 servings.

Smoked Salmon Bagel

THIS NEW YORK DELI-STYLE FRENCH TOAST MAKES A GREAT BRUNCH FOR A LAZY DAY.

3 large eggs
1 cup milk
1/2 teaspoon salt
3 savory day-old bagels
Butter
1/2 cup whipped cream cheese
3 tablespoons minced fresh dill
6 ounces sliced smoked
  Nova Scotia–style salmon
6 tablespoons minced fresh
  flat-leaf parsley

In a pie pan or other shallow pan, whisk together the eggs, milk and salt. Cut bagels in half and soak each slice in egg mixture for about 1 minute on each side. Heat a little butter in a small frying pan over medium-high heat. Cover and cook each bagel half for 2 to 3 minutes on each side, or until lightly browned. Remove cooked slices and put on individual plates; cool to room temperature. Spread a thick layer of cream cheese on one side of each bagel slice. Sprinkle 1/2 tablespoon dill over cream cheese. Place a slice or two of salmon on top, cutting to fit so that the slices hang slightly over sides of bagel. Sprinkle 1 tablespoon parsley over salmon. Makes 6 servings.

Parmesan Pecan Crusted Sticks

THESE ARE THE TASTIEST BREAD STICKS YOU'LL EVER DIP INTO SOUP!

4 large eggs

1 cup cream

4 tablespoons honey

6 tablespoons Dijon mustard

1/2 teaspoon salt

1 cup ground or finely
   diced pecans

1/2 cup toasted breadcrumbs

1/2 cup grated Parmesan cheese

4 tablespoons dried parsley flakes

8 thick slices day-old firm
   white bread

Butter

In a pie pan or other shallow pan, whisk together the eggs, cream, honey, mustard and salt. In another pie pan, mix together the pecans, breadcrumbs, Parmesan cheese and parsley. Dip bread first in egg mixture until well soaked on each side and then in nut mixture, pressing firmly and turning over until well coated. Heat a little butter in a small frying pan over medium-high heat. Cover and cook about 3 minutes, or until well browned and crisp. Cut each slice into 3 or 4 strips. Serve sticks with hot soup for dipping. Makes 4 servings.

Kentucky Hot Browns

THIS SOUTHERN FAVORITE OF BREAD, MEATS AND CHEESE SAUCE COMES
TOGETHER IN A SNAP.

3 large eggs
3 cups milk, divided
2 teaspoons salt, divided
8 slices day-old firm white bread
8 (1/4-inch-thick) slices
    cooked turkey
3 tablespoons butter
2 tablespoons flour
4 ounces extra sharp
    white cheddar cheese, grated
1/2 cup grated Parmesan cheese
1/4 teaspoon nutmeg
1 teaspoon white pepper
4 large ripe tomatoes, sliced
    1/4 inch thick
8 slices bacon, cooked and crumbled

In a pie pan or other shallow pan, mix together eggs, 1/2 cup milk and 1 teaspoon salt. Soak bread slices in egg mixture for 30 second on each side. Cook, covered, in a frying pan sprayed with nonstick cooking spray until lightly browned on each side, about 2 to 3 minutes. Place cooked slices on a baking sheet that has been sprayed with nonstick cooking spray. Place a turkey slice on top of each bread slice; set aside. In a saucepan, melt butter over medium-high heat and then stir in flour; cook 1 minute, stirring constantly. Whisk in remaining milk and simmer until thickened, about 3 to 4 minutes. Stir in cheeses, remaining salt, nutmeg and pepper; remove from heat. Ladle sauce over turkey on bread. Place in oven and broil 3 to 5 minutes, or until top is golden brown. Spread tomato slices and bacon on top. Makes 8 servings.

Desserts

Cookie-Crusted Sundaes

THE COOKIE CRUMBS FORM A SWEET AND CRUNCHY CRUST FOR THE FRENCH TOAST SLICES, MAKING A PERFECT BASE FOR SUNDAE TOPPINGS.

3 large eggs
1 cup half-and-half
1 teaspoon vanilla
1/2 teaspoon salt
6 large snickerdoodle, gingersnap
    or sugar cookies
6 (1-inch-thick) slices day-old
    challah or French bread
6 scoops ice cream
Caramel or chocolate syrup
Whipped cream
Chopped nuts
Maraschino cherries

In a pie pan or other shallow pan, mix together the eggs, half-and-half, vanilla and salt. Whirl cookies in a food processor until fine crumbs and then spread on a plate. Cut bread slices into circles or other festive shapes, approximately 4 inches in diameter. Dip each side of bread first in egg mixture and then in cookie crumbs. Place bread in a small frying pan sprayed with nonstick cooking spray over medium heat. Cover and cook for 1 to 2 minutes on each side, or until lightly browned; cool to room temperature. Place each slice on a plate and then top with ice cream and your favorite sundae ingredients. Makes 6 servings.

Bread Pudding

THE MARRIAGE OF FRENCH TOAST AND BREAD PUDDING GIVES THIS CLASSIC DESSERT A RICH AND CREAMY TEXTURE THAT CAN'T BE BEAT.

8 cups day-old French bread (1-inch cubes)
1/4 cup butter, melted
4 large eggs plus 2 egg yolks
3/4 cup sugar
4 cups half-and-half
1 tablespoon vanilla
1/2 teaspoon salt
1/2 teaspoon nutmeg
1 cup raisins
1/2 cup diced walnuts
Whipped cream for garnish

Spread bread cubes on a baking sheet, forming a single layer and then brush tops with butter. Bake at 325 degrees for 10 to 12 minutes, or until lightly browned. In a bowl, whisk together the eggs, sugar, half-and-half, vanilla, salt and nutmeg. Toss the bread cubes, raisins and walnuts in the egg mixture. Spread in a 9 x 13-inch baking pan that has been sprayed with nonstick cooking spray. Bake, uncovered, at 325 degrees for 45 to 50 minutes, or until browned on top but still slightly jiggly in the center. Let stand 20 minutes before serving. Serve with a spoonful of whipped cream if desired. Makes 6 to 8 servings.

Banana Split

FRENCH TOAST GOES RETRO—IMAGINE THIS DESSERT IN A '50S DINER!

1 jar (10 ounces) maraschino
   cherries, drained
8 ounces cream cheese, softened
1/2 cup powdered sugar
3 large eggs
2/3 cup milk
1 teaspoon vanilla
1/2 teaspoon salt
12 (1/2-inch-thick) slices day-old
   challah or French bread
3 bananas
6 scoops ice cream
Chocolate syrup for garnish

Reserve 6 cherries with stems for garnish; dice the remaining cherries. Mix diced cherries with cream cheese and powdered sugar with a spoon. In a pie pan or other shallow pan, whisk together the eggs, milk, vanilla and salt. Dip both sides of bread in egg mixture. Heat a small frying pan sprayed with nonstick cooking spray over medium-high heat. Cover and cook soaked bread for 1 to 2 minutes on each side, or until lightly browned. Remove from heat and chill 30 minutes, or until cold. On a plate, layer a slice of French toast, 1/3 cup cream cheese mixture, half a banana, sliced, and another slice of French toast. Top with a scoop of ice cream, drizzle with chocolate syrup and place a reserved cherry on top. Makes 6 servings.

Fruit Crisp

FRENCH TOAST CRUMBLES MAKE A GREAT CRUNCHY TOPPING FOR FRUIT—
JUST ADD A SCOOP OF WHIPPED CREAM TO SEAL THE DEAL.

6 large eggs

1 cup milk

1 teaspoon vanilla

1/2 teaspoon salt

*8 to 10 (1/2-inch-thick) slices
    day-old challah or French bread*

*2 cans (21 ounces each)
    cherry pie filling*

*1 can (20 ounces) crushed
    pineapple, with liquid*

1 cup diced pecans

1/2 cup sugar

1 teaspoon cinnamon

In a pie pan or other shallow pan, whisk together the eggs, milk, vanilla and salt. Soak each bread slice in egg mixture for 30 seconds on each side, or until soaked through. Heat a small frying pan sprayed with nonstick spray over medium-high heat. Cook soaked bread in pan 2 to 3 minutes on each side, or until well browned; cool to room temperature. Very finely dice the cooled French toast slices. Spread on a baking sheet in a single layer and bake at 400 degrees for 10 to 12 minutes, or until dried and crisp. In a 3- to 4-quart casserole dish, stir together the cherry pie filling, pineapple and pecans. Toss the French toast bits in sugar and cinnamon and then spread over fruit mixture. Bake at 400 degrees for 30 to 40 minutes, or until cooked through and bubbly on edges. Garnish with whipped topping if desired. Makes 6 to 8 servings.

Chocolate Decadence Stacks

THESE SWEET AND CREAMY CONCOCTIONS ARE A CHOCOLATE LOVER'S DREAM.

1 cup heavy cream, whipped

1/2 cup sugar

8 ounces whipped cream cheese, room temperature

1 teaspoon vanilla

1/2 cup plus 1 tablespoon gourmet cocoa powder, divided

3 large eggs

1 cup milk

1/2 teaspoon salt

12 (1/2-inch-thick) slices day-old angel food cake

8 ounces dark Swiss chocolate, grated

Using a hand mixer, mix the whipped cream, sugar, cream cheese, vanilla and 1/2 cup cocoa powder in a bowl; chill. In a pie pan or other shallow pan, whisk together the eggs, milk, remaining cocoa powder and salt. Soak cake slices in egg mixture for about 30 seconds on each side. Heat a small frying pan sprayed with nonstick cooking spray to medium heat. Place soaked cake slices in pan and cover and cook for 2 to 3 minutes on each side, or until lightly browned; remove and cool to slightly warm. Toast slices in a toaster and then cool to room temperature. Place a cake slice on a plate and spread a thick layer of cream cheese mixture over top. Sprinkle 1 tablespoon grated chocolate over cream cheese and then repeat for a second layer. Makes 6 servings.

Pudding Stuffed

THIS FRENCH TOAST DESSERT PROVES THAT ANY DESSERT IS BETTER WITH RICH, CREAMY PUDDING IN THE MIDDLE!

4 large eggs

1/2 cup cream

1 tablespoon cinnamon

1/4 cup sugar

1 teaspoon vanilla

1/2 teaspoon salt

6 (1 1/2-inch-thick) slices day-old French bread

1 small box instant pudding mix, any flavor

1 1/2 cups very cold milk

Any specialty syrup (see pages 120–126)

In a bowl, whisk together the eggs, cream, cinnamon, sugar, vanilla and salt until frothy. Pour half of the egg mixture into a 9 x 13-inch pan. Place bread slices in pan, completely filling pan. Pour remaining egg mixture over bread and then let soak for 20 minutes. Heat a small frying pan sprayed with nonstick cooking spray over medium-high heat. Cover and cook the soaked bread slices in frying pan for 2 to 3 minutes on each side, or until lightly browned. Chill bread slices for 1 to 2 hours. Mix together pudding mix and milk as directed on box. Remove bread from refrigerator and slice in half partway through lengthwise, forming a pocket in the middle. Fill with two heaping tablespoons pudding and then serve drizzled with a specialty syrup. Makes 6 servings.

Lemony
Blueberry Cobbler

ALL THE TASTE OF CLASSIC BLUEBERRY COBBLER IN A FRENCH TOAST DISH!

6 large eggs

1 cup liquid vanilla coffee creamer

8 cups cubed day-old French
   bread (about 1-inch cubes)

6 cups fresh or frozen blueberries

3 tablespoons cornstarch

1/2 cup sugar

2 tablespoons fresh-squeezed
   lemon juice

1 teaspoon lemon zest

In a bowl, whisk together the eggs and coffee creamer. Add bread cubes, tossing until evenly coated; set aside. (Toss with a spoon occasionally to make sure liquid is evenly absorbed.) Toss berries with cornstarch, sugar, lemon juice and lemon zest and then place in a 4-quart baking dish. Spread soaked bread cubes over top, completely covering surface. Bake at 400 degrees for 30 to 40 minutes, or until cooked through and bubbly around the edges. Serve topped with whipped cream or ice cream, if desired. Makes 6 to 8 servings.

Seven-Layer Strawberry Torte

THIS SPECTACULAR TREAT IS AN EASY BUT ELEGANT TWIST ON EVERYONE'S FAVORITE DESSERT—STRAWBERRY SHORTCAKE.

8 cups sliced fresh strawberries

1 cup sugar, divided

3 large eggs

1 cup milk

1/2 teaspoon salt

2 teaspoons vanilla, divided

6 slices pita bread
   (8-inch diameter)

2 cups heavy cream

In a bowl, mix strawberries with 1/2 cup sugar and set aside. In a pie pan or other shallow pan, whisk together the eggs, milk, salt and 1 teaspoon vanilla. Soak each pita in egg mixture for about 2 minutes, or until softened. Heat a 9-inch frying pan sprayed with nonstick cooking spray to medium-high heat. Cover and cook soaked pitas 1 to 2 minutes on each side, or until lightly browned. Cool and then sprinkle 1 teaspoon sugar on each pita. Whip cream with remaining vanilla and sugar until thick and peaks form. Place a pita on a 10- to 12-inch serving platter. Spread 2/3 cup whipped cream and 1 cup sliced strawberries over top. Repeat layers to make one tall stack, ending with whipped cream and then a strawberry on top to garnish. Refrigerate 1 hour before serving. Makes 6 to 8 servings.

Molten Chocolate Pistachio

THIS DECADENT CHOCOLATE DESSERT YIELDS A SURPRISE WHEN WARM CHOCOLATE OOZES FROM THE FIRST BITE.

8 ounces extra-fine baking
    chocolate, grated
    (60 percent cocoa)
2 cups heavy cream, divided
1/2 cup sugar
16 thick slices day-old firm
    white bread, crusts removed
1 cup ground or very finely
    diced pistachios, divided
4 large eggs
1 teaspoon vanilla
1/2 teaspoon salt
2 cups chocolate wafer
    cookie crumbs
Chocolate syrup

Put chocolate in a small bowl. In a saucepan, bring 1 cup cream and sugar to a boil. Pour boiling cream mixture into chocolate and stir until melted; chill for 2 hours or until firm. Roll chocolate mixture into 8 balls. Flatten balls with hands until they are about 1/4- to 1/2-inch-thick disks. Place disks on 8 bread slices. Evenly sprinkle 1/2 cup pistachios over chocolate disks. Top with remaining bread slices and then press lightly to seal. In a pie pan or other shallow pan, whisk together remaining cream, eggs, vanilla and salt. Mix together cookie crumbs and remaining pistachios and then spread mixture on a plate. Dip chocolate sandwiches first in egg mixture and then in crumbs. Place coated sandwiches on an oiled baking sheet. Bake at 425 degrees for 8 minutes; turn over and bake 5 minutes more. Remove from oven and serve hot, drizzled with chocolate syrup. Makes 8 servings.

Crème Brûlée

THIS DESSERT HAS THAT CLASSIC SUGAR-CRUSTED TASTE EVERYONE LOVES.

1/4 cup butter
1/2 cup brown sugar
2 tablespoons corn syrup
6 (1 1/2-inch-thick) slices day-old
  challah bread
5 large eggs
1 1/2 cups cream
1 tablespoon vanilla
1/2 teaspoon salt
6 tablespoons sugar

Melt butter in a small frying pan. Stir in brown sugar and corn syrup and cook until sugar is dissolved, stirring constantly. Pour mixture into a 9 x 13-inch baking pan and then place bread slices on top. In a bowl, whisk together the eggs, cream, vanilla and salt. Pour egg mixture over the bread slices, making sure to saturate all slices. Cover and refrigerate at least 2 hours or overnight. Remove from refrigerator and bring to room temperature, about 30 minutes. Bake, uncovered, at 375 degrees for 40 to 45 minutes, or until puffed and lightly browned. Place each slice on a serving plate. Spread 1 tablespoon sugar on top of each slice. With a kitchen torch, torch the sugar until browned and crisp. Makes 6 slices.

Variation: *If you don't have a kitchen torch, broil on high for about 2 minutes, until browned and crisp, watching carefully not to burn.*

Specialty Syrups
and Sauces

Maple Cream Syrup

1 cup sugar
1/2 cup butter
1/2 cup pure maple syrup
1/4 cup milk or cream

Bring to a simmer sugar, butter, maple syrup and milk or cream. Simmer until sugar is dissolved and syrup is slightly thickened. Serve warm. Store in the refrigerator for up to 2 weeks. Makes 2 cups.

Decadent Vanilla Cream Syrup

1 cup cream
1/2 cup sugar
1 tablespoon flour
4 egg yolks
1 tablespoon vanilla
1 cup vanilla ice cream

Bring cream and sugar to a boil over medium-high heat. In a small bowl, mix together flour, egg yolks and vanilla. Add a few spoonfuls of the boiling cream mixture, and then add the egg yolk mixture to the cream mixture, stirring constantly for 3 minutes. Add vanilla ice cream and continue to cook for another 3 minutes, stirring constantly until thickened. Serve warm. Store in the refrigerator for up to 2 weeks. Makes 2 cups.

Blueberry Syrup

1 cup sugar
1/2 cup corn syrup
1 cup blueberries
1 teaspoon vanilla

In a blender, blend sugar, corn syrup and blueberries. Pour into a small saucepan and bring to a simmer, stirring for 3 minutes. Remove from heat and cool for 5 minutes. Stir in vanilla. Serve warm. Store in the refrigerator for up to 2 weeks. Makes 2 cups.

Raspberry Syrup

1 container (12 ounces)
   frozen apple raspberry
   juice concentrate
3 tablespoons cornstarch
2 cups fresh or frozen
   raspberries

Mix apple raspberry concentrate and cornstarch. Bring mixture to a simmer in a small saucepan, stirring until thickened. Remove from heat and stir in 2 cups fresh or frozen raspberries. Serve warm. Store in the refrigerator for up to 2 weeks. Makes 2 cups.

Cranapple Compote

1/2 cup butter

3 Golden Delicious apples, peeled and diced

1 cup chopped fresh cranberries

1/2 cup sugar

1 container (12 ounces) frozen apple juice concentrate

1/4 cup corn syrup

2 tablespoons brown sugar

In a medium saucepan over medium-high heat, melt butter and sauté apples for 2 minutes. Add cranberries and sugar and stir until cranberries pop, about 2 minutes more. Stir in juice concentrate, corn syrup and brown sugar. Simmer until thickened, about 5 minutes. Remove from heat and cool slightly before serving. Store in the refrigerator for up to 2 weeks. Makes 2 cups.

Chunky Cherry Syrup

1 can (14 ounces) sour pitted cherries, drained and diced

1 cup corn syrup

1/2 cup sugar

Red food coloring, optional

Place cherries in a small saucepan. Add corn syrup and sugar and bring to a full rolling boil. Reduce heat and let simmer 25 to 30 minutes, or until thickened. Turn off heat and add a few drops of red food coloring, if desired. Let cool to warm and serve. Store in the refrigerator for up to 2 weeks. Makes 2 cups.

Fresh Fruit Purée

3 cups fresh fruit or berries
1 teaspoon lemon juice
2 tablespoons pure maple syrup
2 tablespoons light corn syrup
A few tablespoons water,
   if necessary

In blender, blend together the fruit, lemon juice, maple syrup, corn syrup and water, if necessary, to make the right syrup consistency Store in the refrigerator for up to 1 week. Makes 2 cups.

Easy Blender Hollandaise Sauce

3 egg yolks
1 tablespoon lemon juice
1/4 teaspoon salt
1/4 teaspoon white pepper
1/2 cup butter

In a blender, blend egg yolks, lemon juice, salt and white pepper. Melt butter in microwave until sizzling hot. Turn blender on low and slowly pour in all the melted butter. Serve warm. Store in the refrigerator for 3 to 5 days. Makes 1 cup.

Cinnamon Cream Syrup

1 cup sugar
1/2 cup corn syrup
1/2 teaspoon cinnamon
1/2 cup evaporated milk

In a small saucepan, combine sugar, corn syrup and cinnamon. Bring to a boil, stirring for 3 minutes. Remove from heat and cool for 5 minutes. Stir in evaporated milk. Serve warm. Store in the refrigerator for up to 1 week. Makes 2 cups.

Old-Fashioned Buttermilk Syrup

1/2 cup butter
1 1/2 cups sugar
2 tablespoons light corn syrup
3/4 cup buttermilk
2 teaspoons vanilla
1 teaspoon baking soda

Melt butter in a saucepan. Add remaining ingredients and simmer over medium-low heat for 7 to 8 minutes, stirring frequently. Serve warm. Store in the refrigerator for up to 2 weeks. Makes 3 cups.

Citrus Sunshine Syrup

2 tablespoons sugar
1 tablespoon lemon zest
2 tablespoons orange zest
1 1/2 cups corn syrup
2 tablespoons frozen orange
   juice concentrate
2 tablespoons lemon juice
1 cinnamon stick

Mix sugar into zests and let stand at least 30 minutes. Place in a blender and add remaining ingredients except cinnamon stick and blend until smooth, about 1 minute. Pour into a small saucepan over medium heat; add cinnamon stick and simmer for about 20 minutes, stirring every 2 minutes. Store in the refrigerator for up to 2 weeks. Makes 2 cups.

Metric Conversion Chart

Liquid and Dry Measures

U.S.	Canadian	Australian
¼ teaspoon	1 mL	1 ml
½ teaspoon	2 mL	2 ml
1 teaspoon	5 mL	5 ml
1 tablespoon	15 mL	20 ml
¼ cup	50 mL	60 ml
⅓ cup	75 mL	80 ml
½ cup	125 mL	125 ml
⅔ cup	150 mL	170 ml
¾ cup	175 mL	190 ml
1 cup	250 mL	250 ml
1 quart	1 liter	1 litre

Temperature Conversion Chart

Fahrenheit	Celsius
250	120
275	140
300	150
325	160
350	180
375	190
400	200
425	220
450	230
475	240
500	260

Index

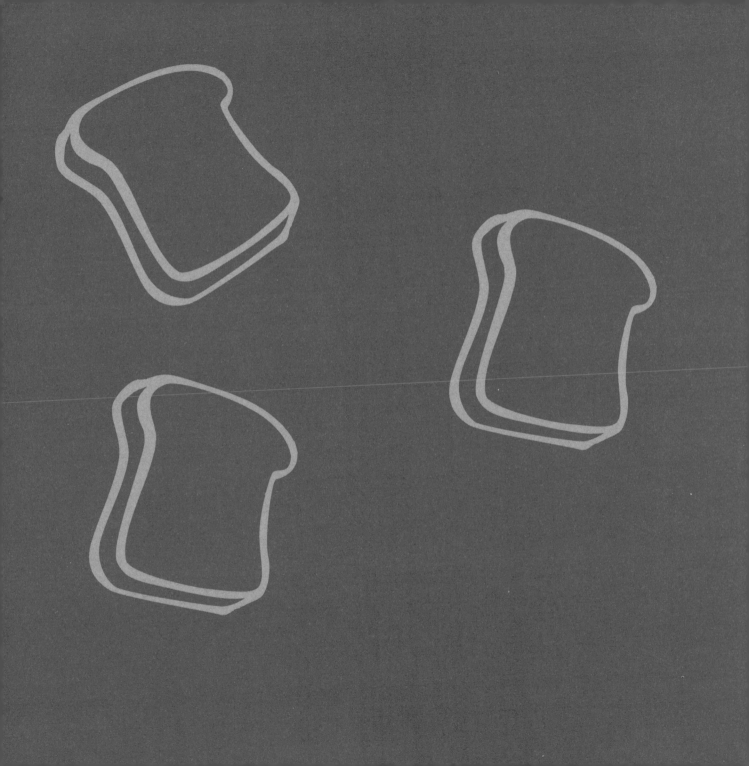